LAUGH-OUT-LOUD JOKES

LAUGH-OUT-LOUD PET JOKES

BY LEONA FOWLER

WINDMILL BOOKS

Published in 2026 by Windmill Books, an Imprint of Rosen Publishing
2544 Clinton St., Buffalo, NY 14224

First Edition

Editor: Caitie McAneney
Book Design: Claire Zimmermann

Photo Credits: Cover, p.1 (child laughing) MillaF/Shutterstock.com; series art (paper texture) OanaGherghe2/Shutterstock.com; series art (illustrations throughout) Nadzin/Shutterstock.com; series art (illustrations) cover (pet food and treats), pp. 8, 10, 12 (pink bird), 16, 18, 22, 23 Look_Studio/Shutterstock.com; p. 5 Masarik/Shutterstock.com; p. 7 New Africa/Shutterstock.com; p. 9 lara-sh/Shutterstock.com; p. 11 leungchopan/Shutterstock.com; p. 13 Daria_vg/Shutterstock.com; p. 15 KAZLOVA IRYNA/Shutterstock.com; p. 17 merkulovstudio/Shutterstock.com; p. 19 Kurit afshen/Shutterstock.com; p. 21 Anna Averianova/Shutterstock.com.

Some of the images in this book illustrate individuals who are models. The depictions do not imply actual situations or events.

Library of Congress Cataloging-in-Publication Data

Names: Fowler, Leona, author.
Title: Laugh-out-loud pet jokes / Leona Fowler.
Description: Buffalo : Windmill Books, 2026. | Series: Laugh-out-loud jokes | Includes index.
Identifiers: LCCN 2025007044 (print) | LCCN 2025007045 (ebook) | ISBN 9781538399170 (library binding) | ISBN 9781538399163 (paperback) | ISBN 9781538399187 (ebook)
Subjects: LCSH: Pets–Juvenile humor. | Wit and humor, Juvenile.
Classification: LCC PN6231.P42 F69 2026 (print) | LCC PN6231.P42 (ebook) | DDC 818/.602–dc23/eng/20250312
LC record available at https://lccn.loc.gov/2025007044
LC ebook record available at https://lccn.loc.gov/2025007045

Manufactured in the United States of America

CPSIA Compliance Information: Batch #CSWM26. For further information, contact Rosen Publishing at 1-800-237-9932

CONTENTS

Words in the glossary appear in **bold** the first time they are used in the text.

DOGGONE IT!

What kind of dog sneezes the most?

ACHOO-WAWA!

What do you call a meditating dog?

AWARE WOLF.

What kind of dog loves winter?

A CHILI DOG.

Why did the dog do great in school?

SHE WAS THE TEACHER'S PET.

FUN FACT!

Dogs are the most common pet in the United States. More than 65 million U.S. households have a dog!

CATS WITH ATTITUDE

Where do cats go to dance?

THE FUR BALL.

What did the alien say to the kitten?

"TAKE ME TO YOUR LITTER."

What do you call a big cat that isn't telling the truth?

A LION.

What do you call an old tomcat?

GRAND-PAW.

FUN FACT!

A litter is a bunch of kittens born to the same mother. Mother cats usually have between four and six kittens.

WACKY RODENTS

Why wouldn't the hamster stop running on its wheel?

IT WAS ON A ROLL!

Where do hamsters go on vacation?

HAMSTERDAM.

What's a rodent's favorite dessert?

MICE CREAM.

What's a rabbit's favorite dance?

HIP-HOP.

FUN FACT!

Some rodents make good pets! People keep mice, rats, gerbils, guinea pigs, rabbits, and hamsters.

SASSY SNAKES

How do pet snakes say goodnight?

THEY GIVE YOU A GOODNIGHT HISS.

What kind of snake is great at baking?

A PIE-THON.

What kind of reptile has the best personality?

A SNAKE CHARMER.

How are snakes and computers alike?

THEY BOTH HAVE MEGA-BITES.

FUN FACT!

Ball pythons are the most common pet snakes in the United States. They are good for beginner snake owners.

BIRD BRAINS

Why should you buy a pet bird?

BECAUSE THEY'RE CHEEP!

When do you need to bring a sick bird to the vet?

WHEN IT NEEDS TWEETMENT.

How do birds work out?

THEY EGG-CERSIZE.

What do parrots like to play?

HIDE AND SPEAK.

FUN FACT!

Parrots use speech to fit into their **flock.** They will also use speech to fit in with your family! They are great at **mimicking** what people say.

A HORSE, OF COURSE

What happened when the horse fell down?

HE COULDN'T GIDDY-UP!

How do horses say hello?

"HAY, NEIGH-BOR!"

Where do you take your sick horse?

THE HORSE-PITAL.

What's a horse's favorite kind of book?

A TALE OF WHOA.

FUN FACT!

Horses can sleep standing up!

FUNNY FISH

How can you talk to a fish?

YOU DROP IT A LINE.

Why can't you eat a clownfish?

THEY TASTE FUNNY!

What do fish need to keep them healthy?

VITAMIN SEA.

Where do fish go on vacation?

FINLAND.

FUN FACT!

People keep both freshwater and saltwater fish as pets. Good starter fish are goldfish, betas, and neon tetras.

LIZARD LAUGHS

What did the chameleon say to her daughter on the first day of school?

"DON'T WORRY, YOU'LL BLEND RIGHT IN!"

What's a gecko's favorite movie?

THE LIZARD OF OZ.

What's a bearded dragon's favorite sport?

CRICKET.

Why are lizard jokes so long?

THEY TEND TO DRAGON.

FUN FACT!

Since lizards are cold-blooded, they get their body warmth from their **environment**. Lizard owners need to have tanks with heat lamps.

PETS WITH A TWIST

What do you get when you cross a centipede and a parrot?

A WALKIE TALKIE.

What do you get when you cross a loyal pet and a calculator?

A FRIEND YOU CAN COUNT ON.

What do you get when you cross a dog and a phone?

A GOLDEN RECEIVER.

What happens when you cross a Cocker spaniel, a poodle, and a ghost?

A COCKER-POODLE-BOO!

FUN FACT!

Many dog breeds are mixed with poodles because they don't shed very much, which makes them a good choice for people who are **allergic** to dogs.

GLOSSARY

allergic: To have a sensitivity to usually harmless things in the surroundings, such as dust, pollen, or certain animals.

environment: The conditions that surround a living thing and affect the way it lives.

flock: A group of animals, such as birds.

meditate: To spend time in quiet thinking.

mimic: To copy.

personality: The whole collection of individual emotions and behavior that make one person different from others.

receiver: Equipment for receiving, or letting in, radio or TV broadcasts.

reptile: An animal covered with scales or plates that breathes air, has a backbone, and lays eggs, such as a turtle, snake, lizard, or crocodile.

rodent: A small, furry animal with large front teeth, such as a mouse or rat.

FOR MORE INFORMATION

BOOKS

Klepeis, Alicia. *The History of Pet Cats.* Minneapolis, MN: Jump! Inc., 2024.

O'Daly, Anne. *Birds.* Buffalo, NY: KidHaven Publishing, 2024.

WEBSITES

Dog Jokes
www.ducksters.com/jokes/dogs.php
Enjoy more dog jokes from Ducksters!

Pet Central
kids.nationalgeographic.com/pages/topic/pet-central
Learn more about pets with National Geographic Kids.

INDEX

TITLES IN THIS SERIES

LAUGH-OUT-LOUD **BUG JOKES**

LAUGH-OUT-LOUD **FAIRY TALE JOKES**

LAUGH-OUT-LOUD **GROSS JOKES**

LAUGH-OUT-LOUD **MAGIC JOKES**

LAUGH-OUT-LOUD **PET JOKES**

LAUGH-OUT-LOUD **SCIENCE JOKES**

LAUGH-OUT-LOUD **SPORTS JOKES**

LAUGH-OUT-LOUD **TECH JOKES**

WINDMILL BOOKS™

ISBN: 9781538399163

9 781538 399163